Burke Thumoth, Lady Dorothea Ruggle-Brise

Twelve Scotch and Twelve Irish Airs with Variations

Set for the German Flute Violin or Harpsichord

Burke Thumoth, Lady Dorothea Ruggle-Brise

Twelve Scotch and Twelve Irish Airs with Variations
Set for the German Flute Violin or Harpsichord

ISBN/EAN: 9783337126520

Printed in Europe, USA, Canada, Australia, Japan

Cover: Foto ©Thomas Meinert / pixelio.de

More available books at **www.hansebooks.com**

Twelve Scotch,

and

Twelve Irish

Airs

with

VARIATIONS

Set for the German Flute Violin
or Harpfichord, by

Mr Burk Thumoth

LONDON. Printed for S. A. and P. THOMPSON,
No 75 St Paul's Church Yard.

The Berks of Endermay.

No. I.

Piano

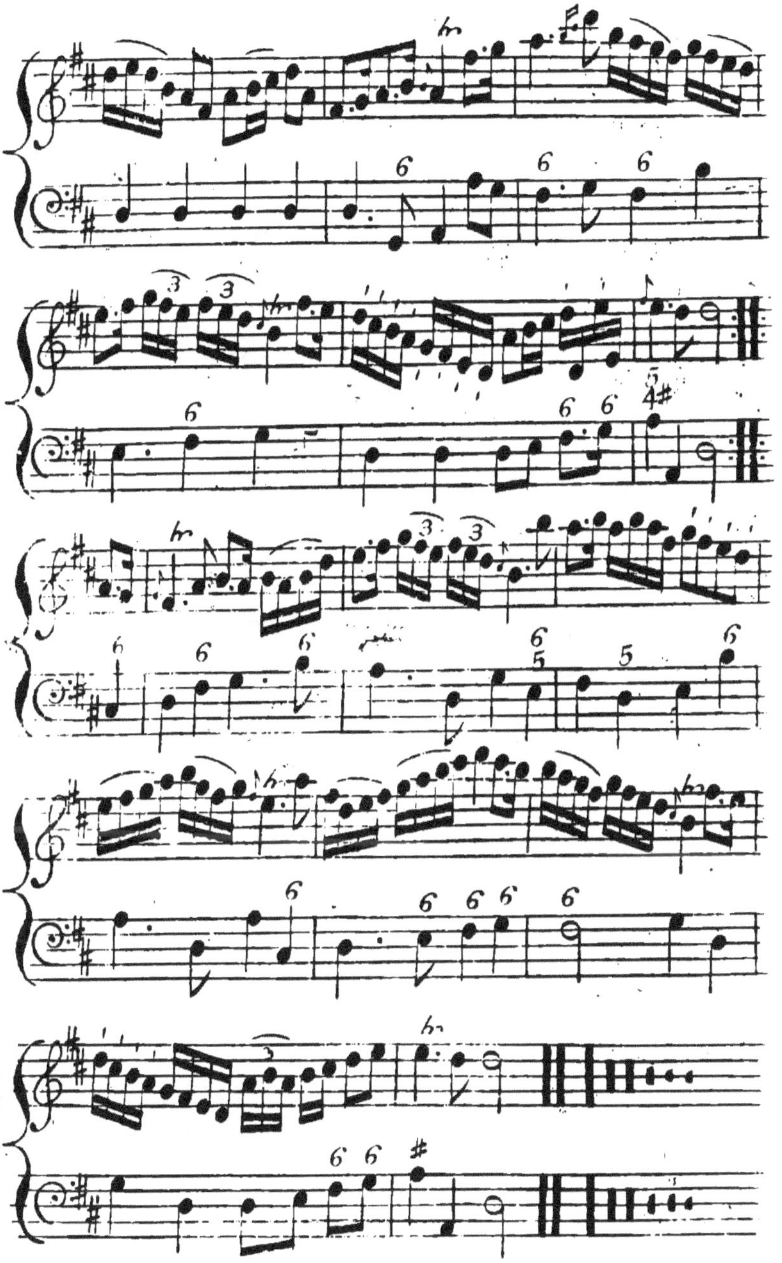

The yellow hair'd Laddie.

N°. II. Slow

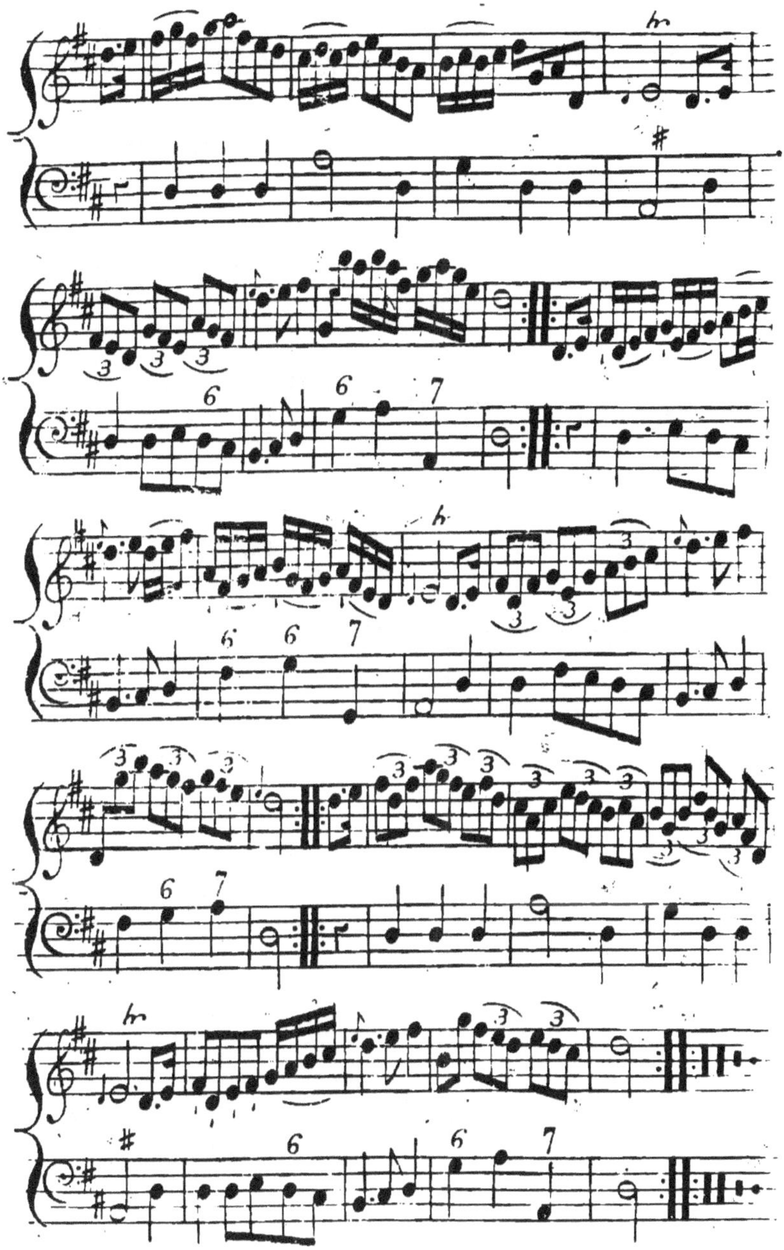

So merry as we twa have been

N.º III.

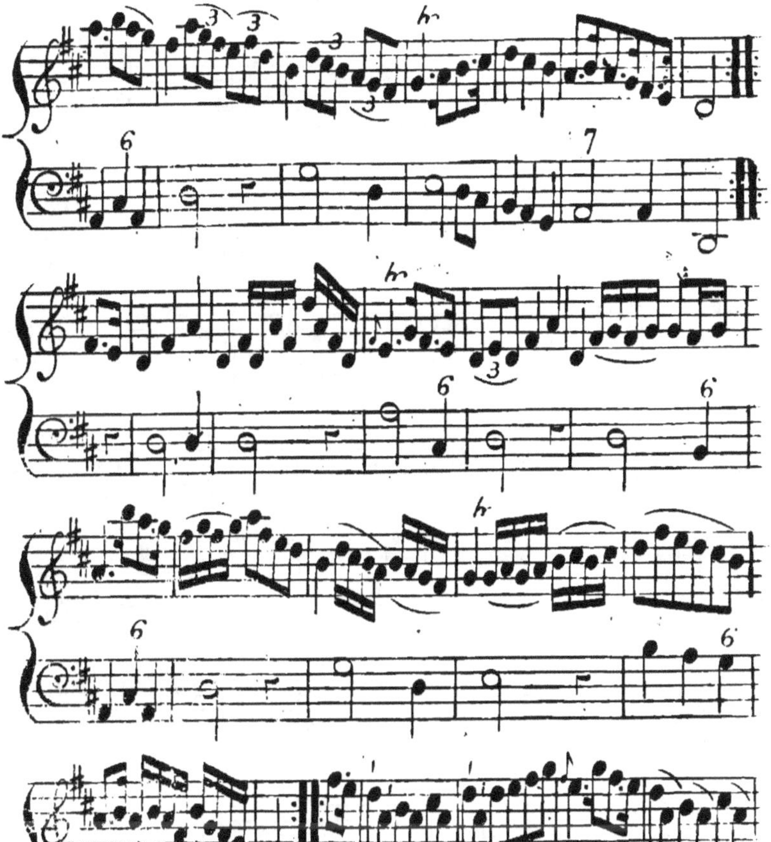
D.C

Mary Scot.

N:º IV.

Slow

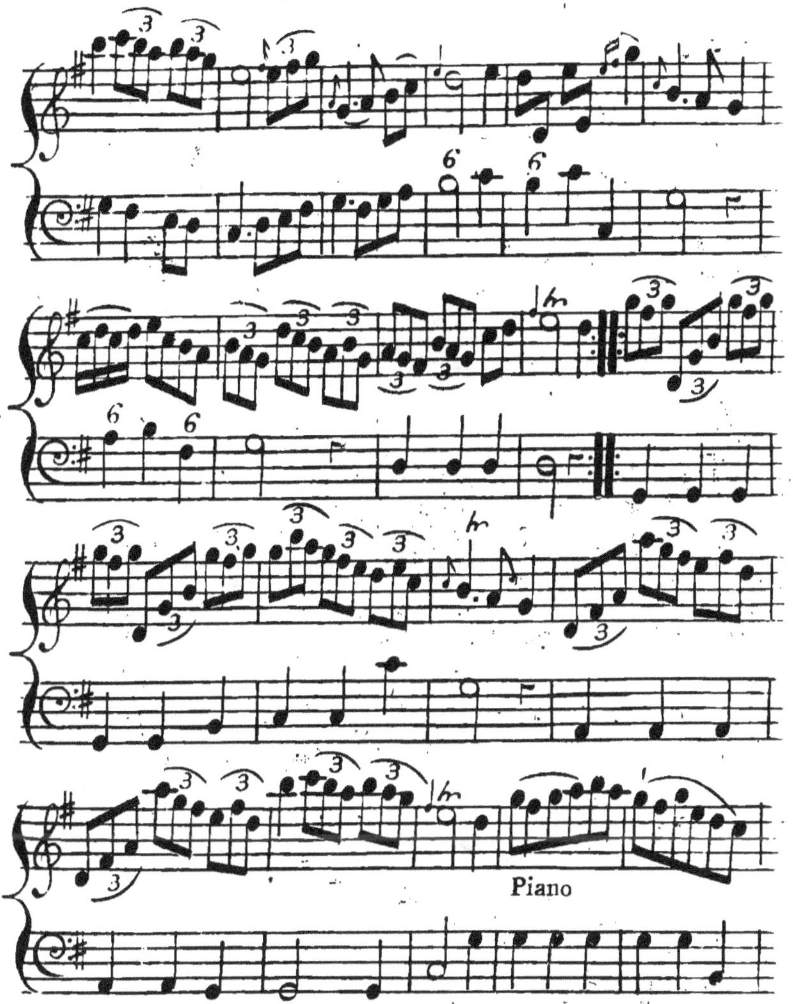
Piano
For

The Lass of Paty's Mill.

N.º V.

Variations

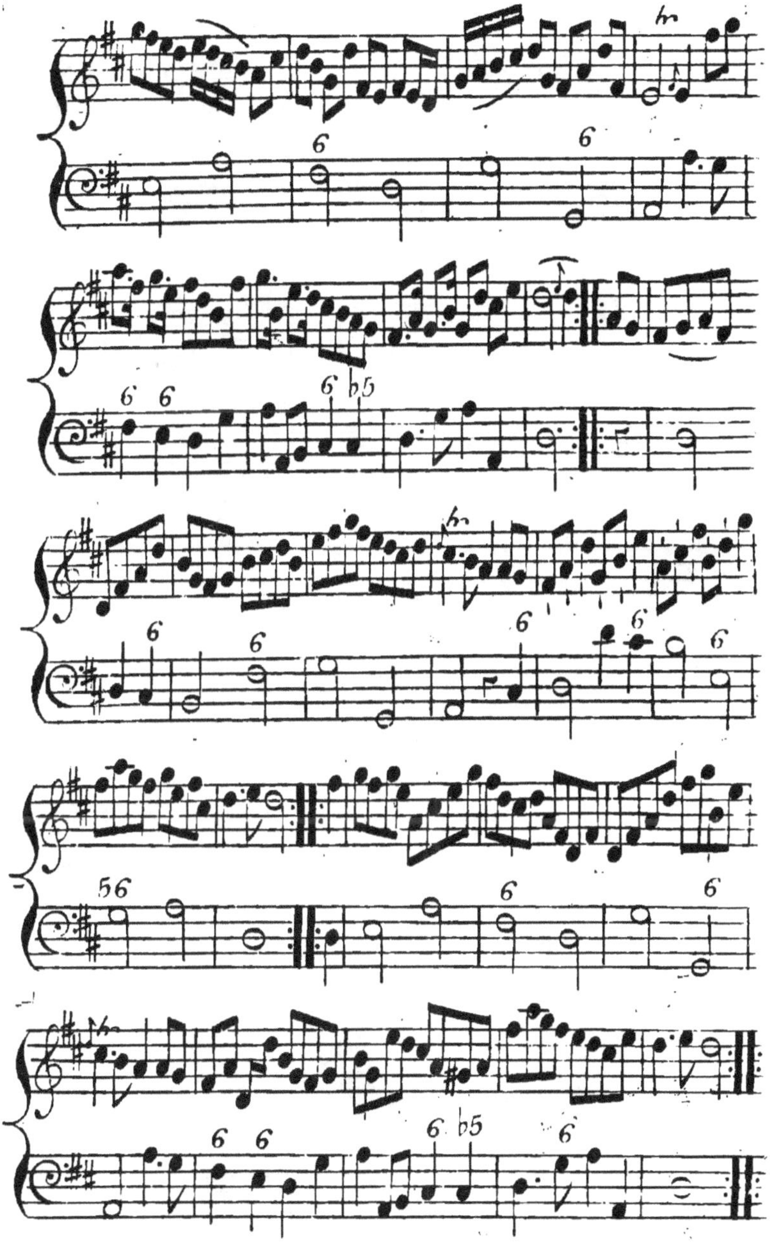

Tweed Side.

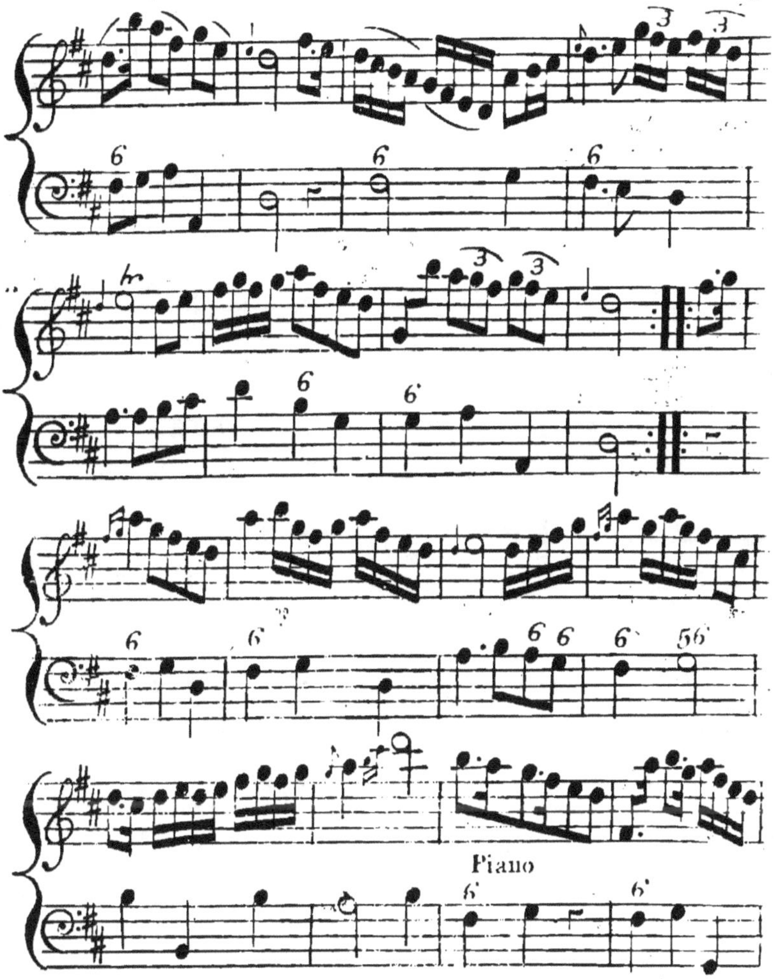
Piano

Tho' for seven long Years.

N.º VII.

Slow

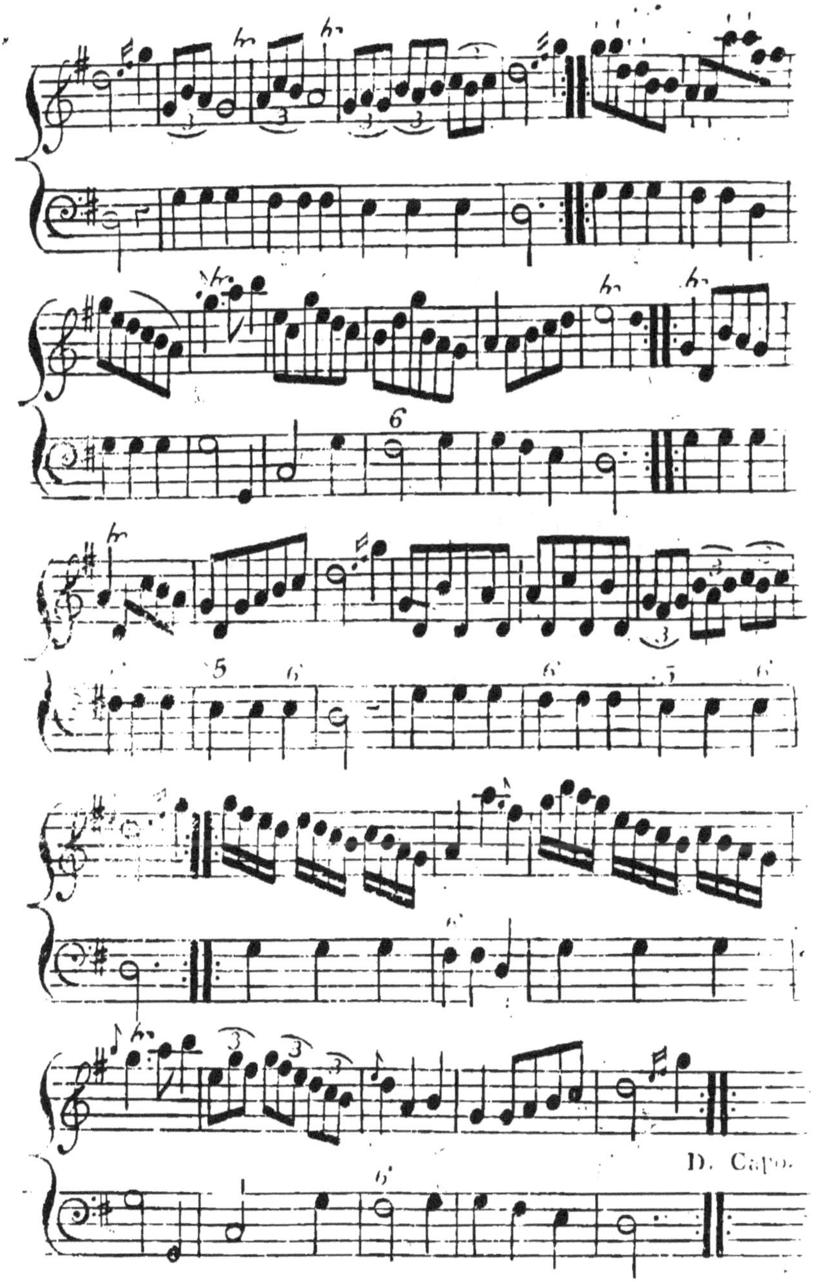
D. Capo

The last time I came o'er the Moor.

Nº VIII.

Slow

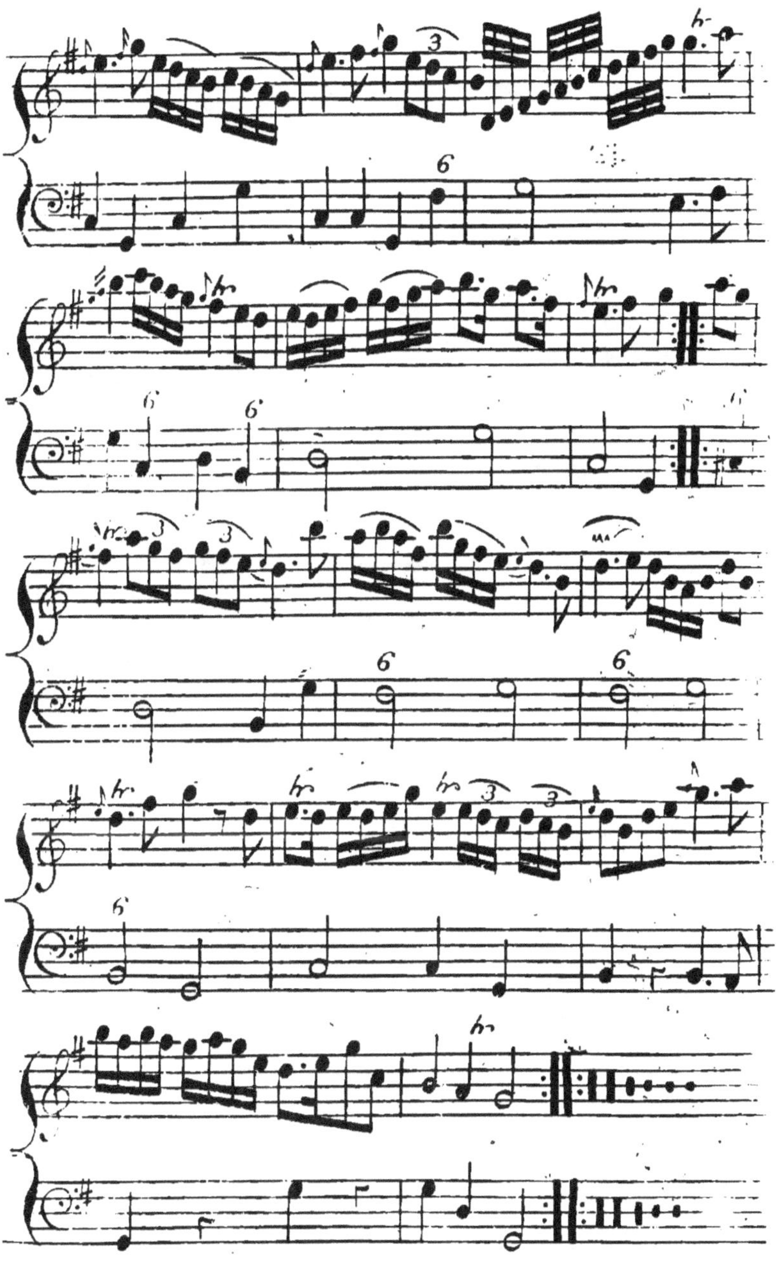

Bonny Jean.

N.º IX.

Allegro

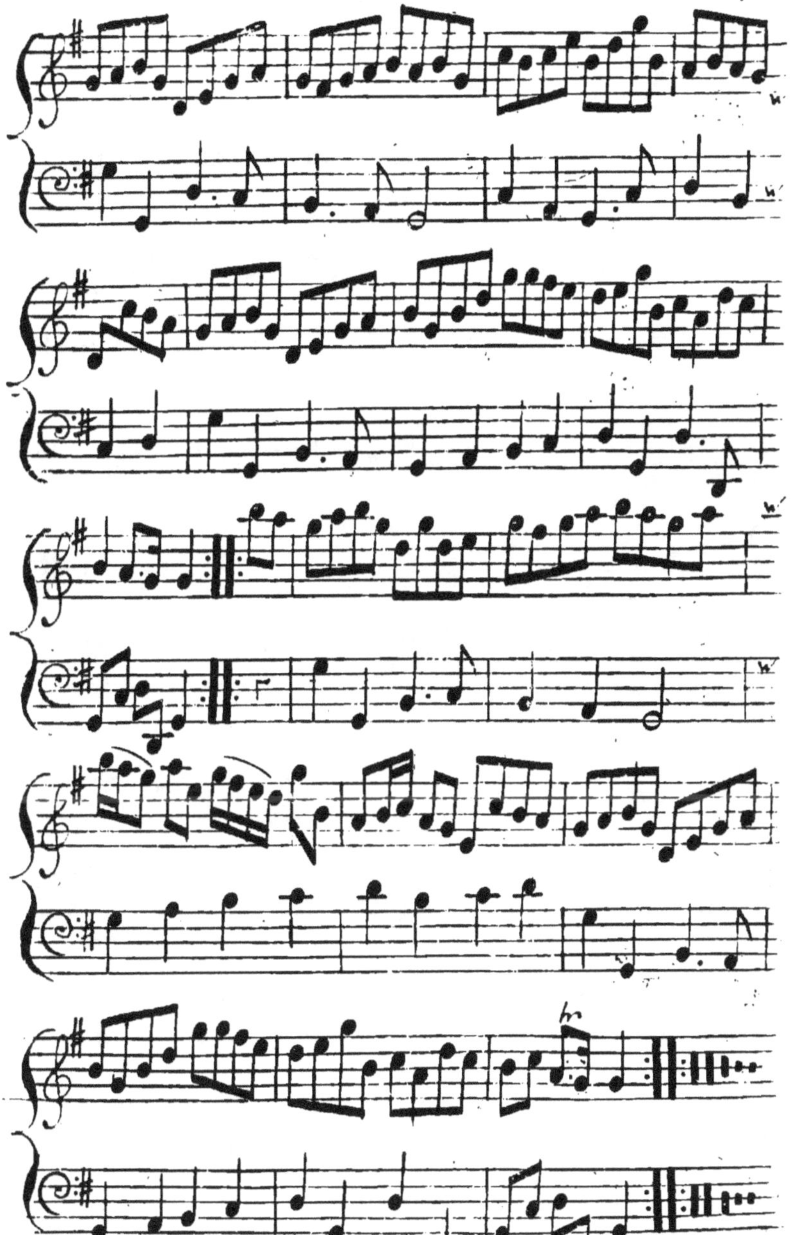

Thro' the Wood Laddie.

N°. X.

Slow

Piano

Variations

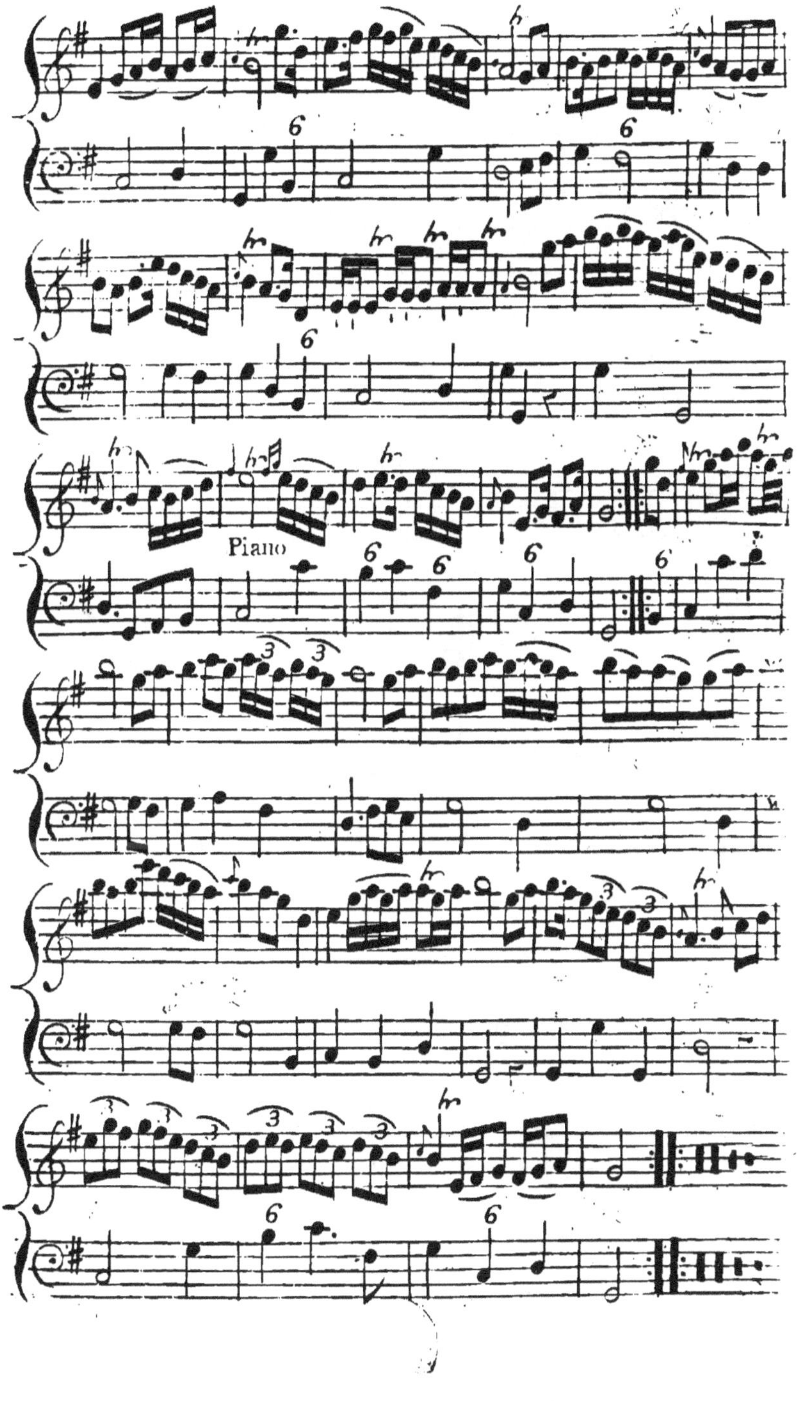
Piano

Corn Riggs are bonny.

N.º XI.

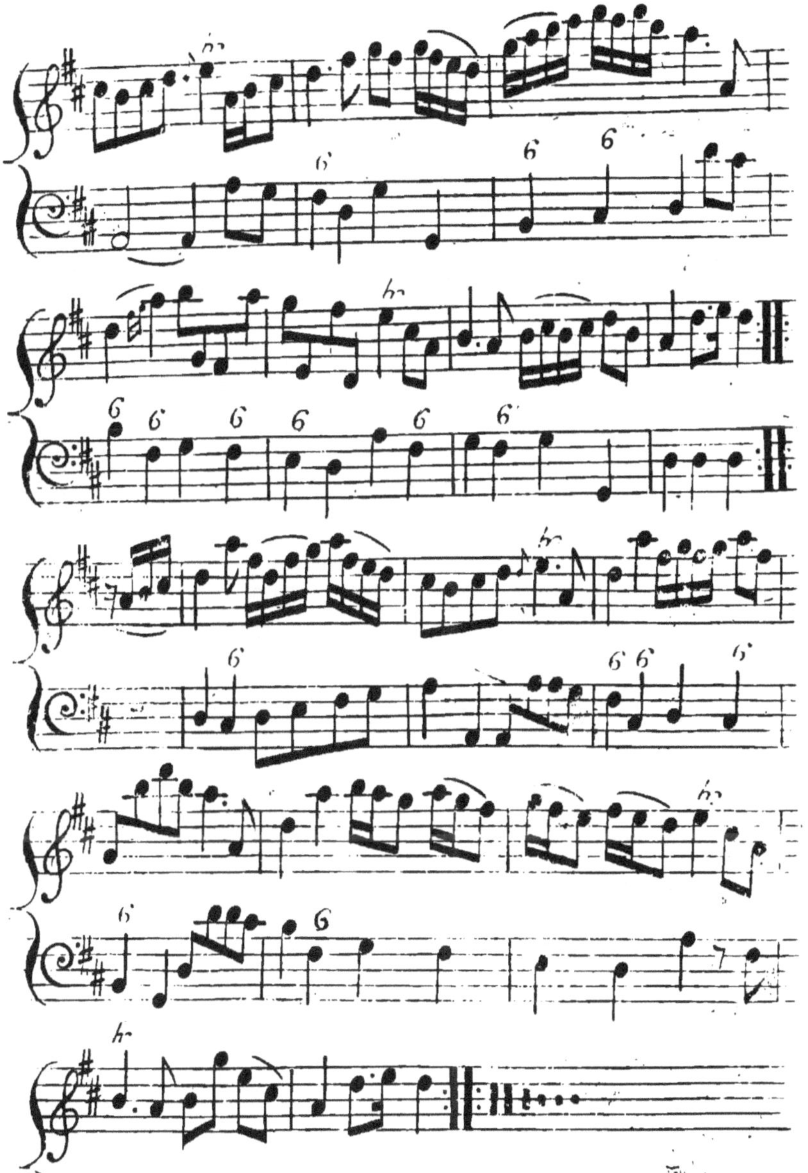

Watuee March

No: XII.

Allegro

Staccata

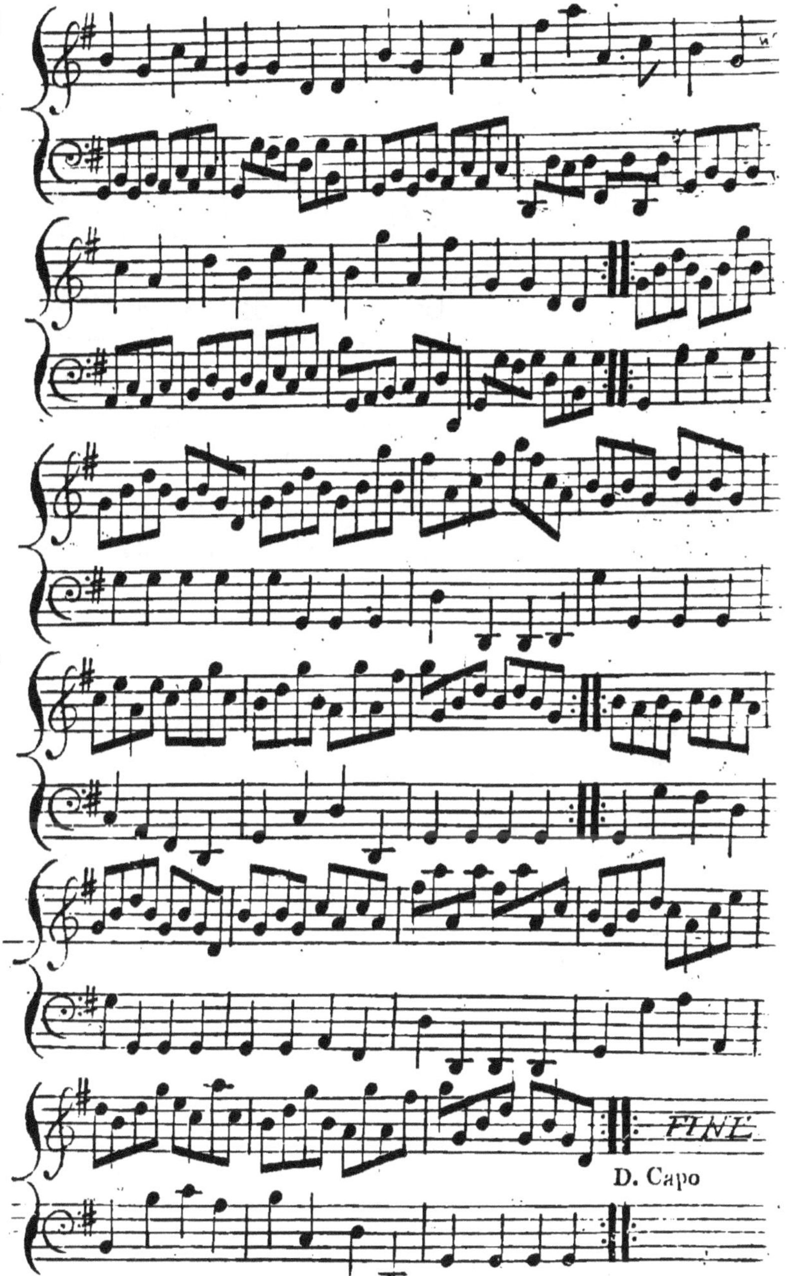
FINE
D. Capo

Ailen Aroon.

No. XIII

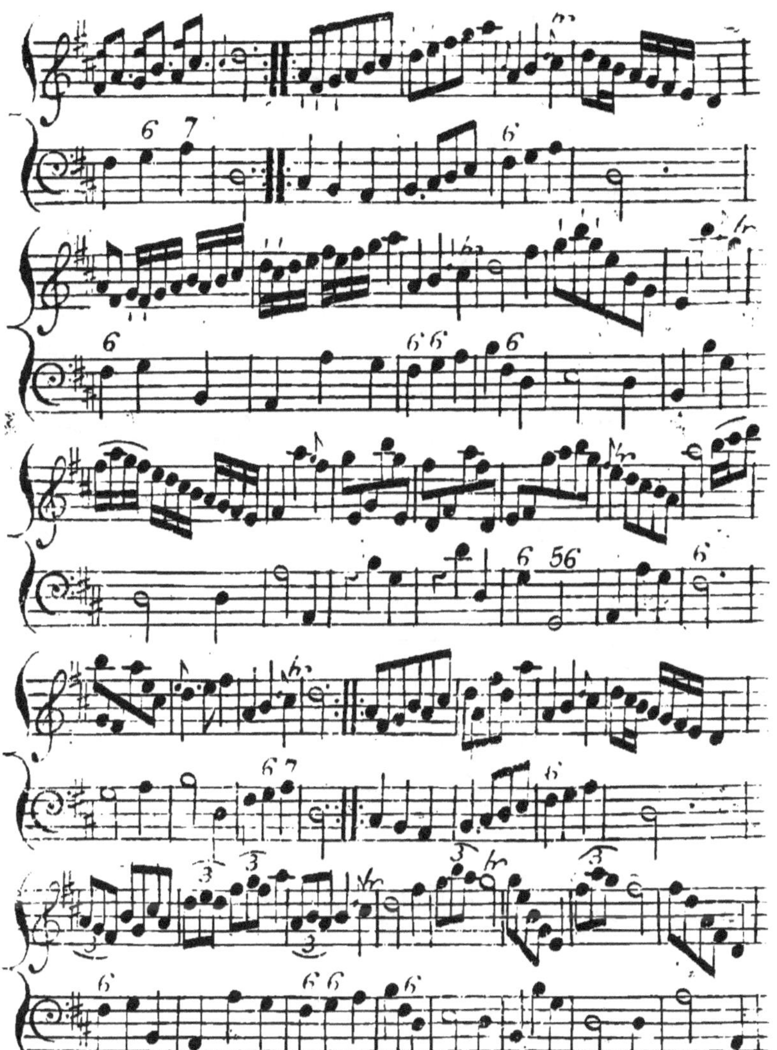
Capo

Yemon O nock

N:XIV

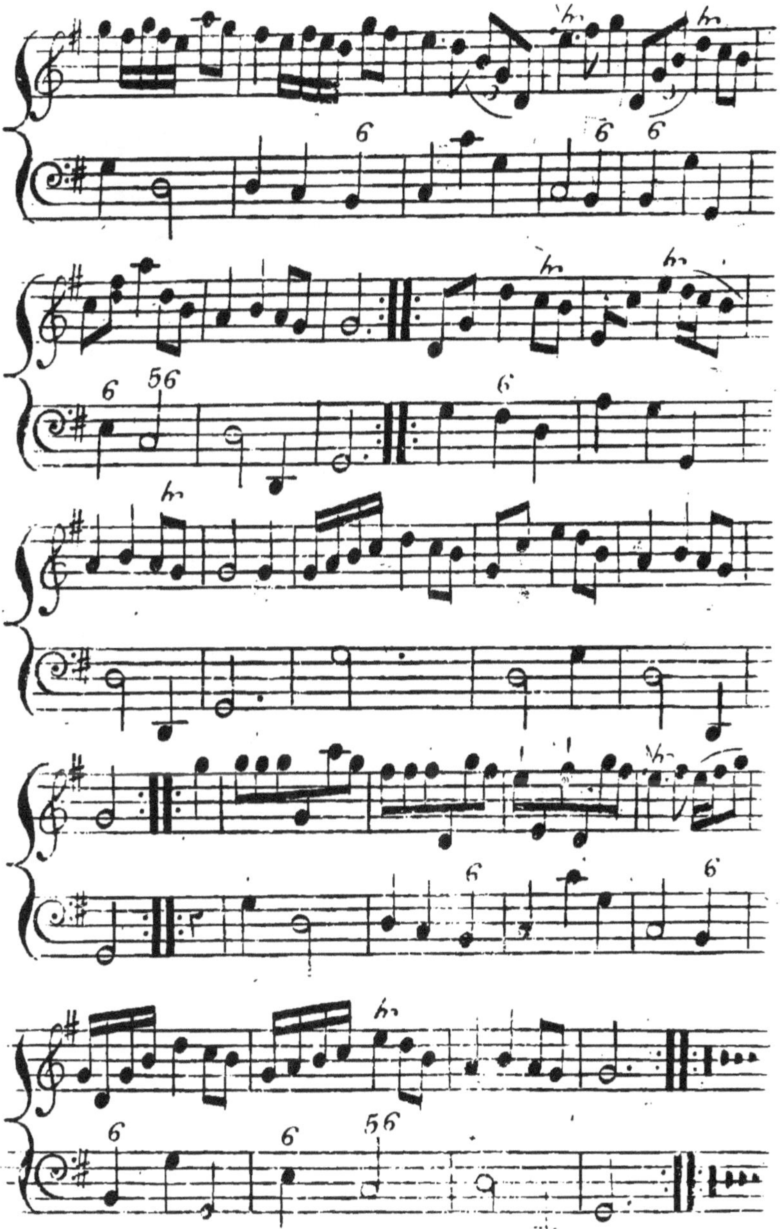

Past one o'Clock.

N.º XV

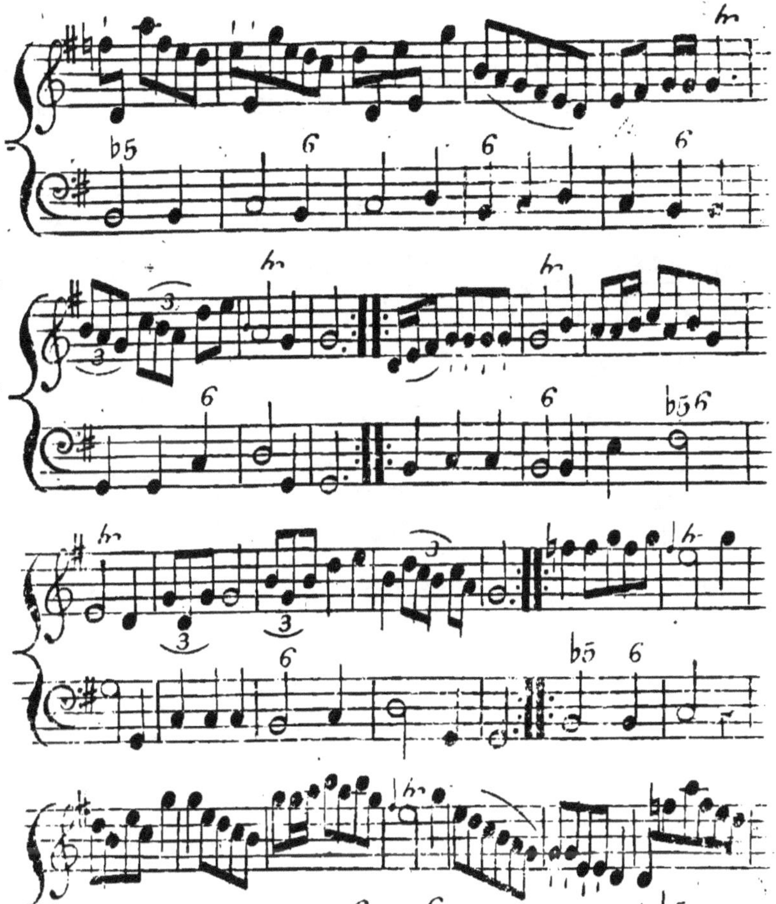

Chiling O-guiry.

N:° XVI

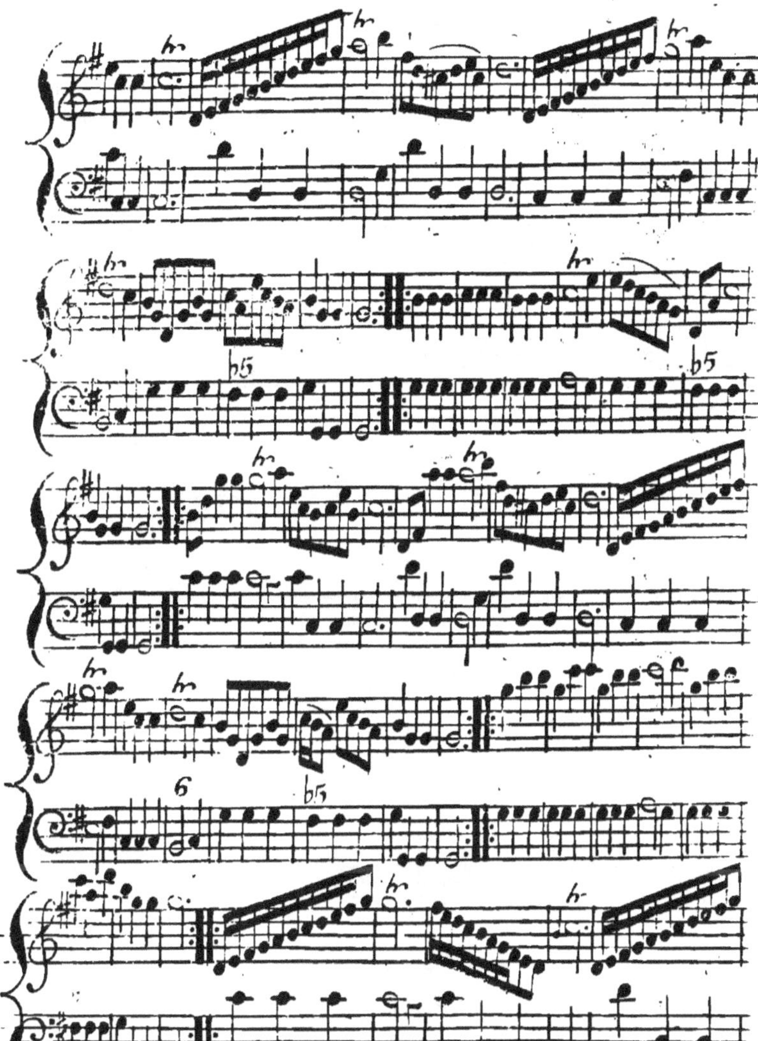
tr
b5
6
3

Slaunt Ri Plulib.

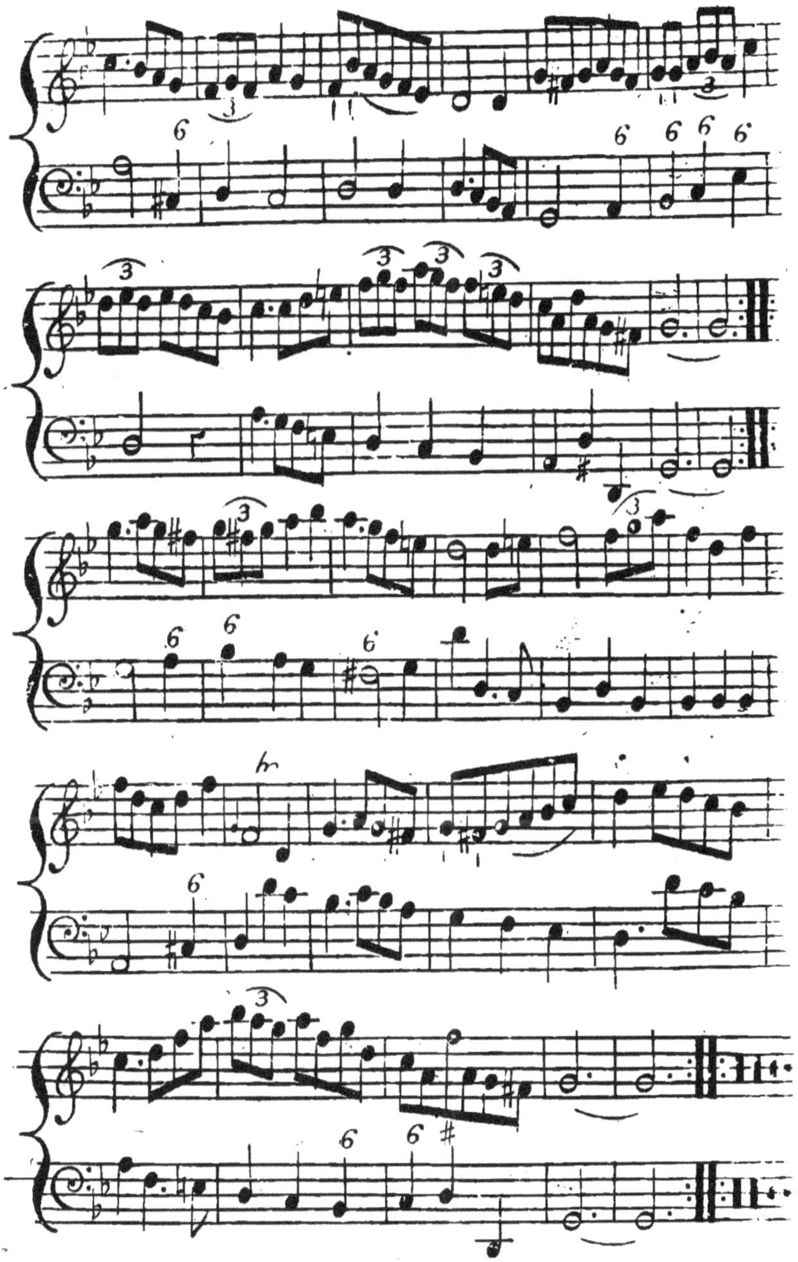

The Major.

N:° XVIII

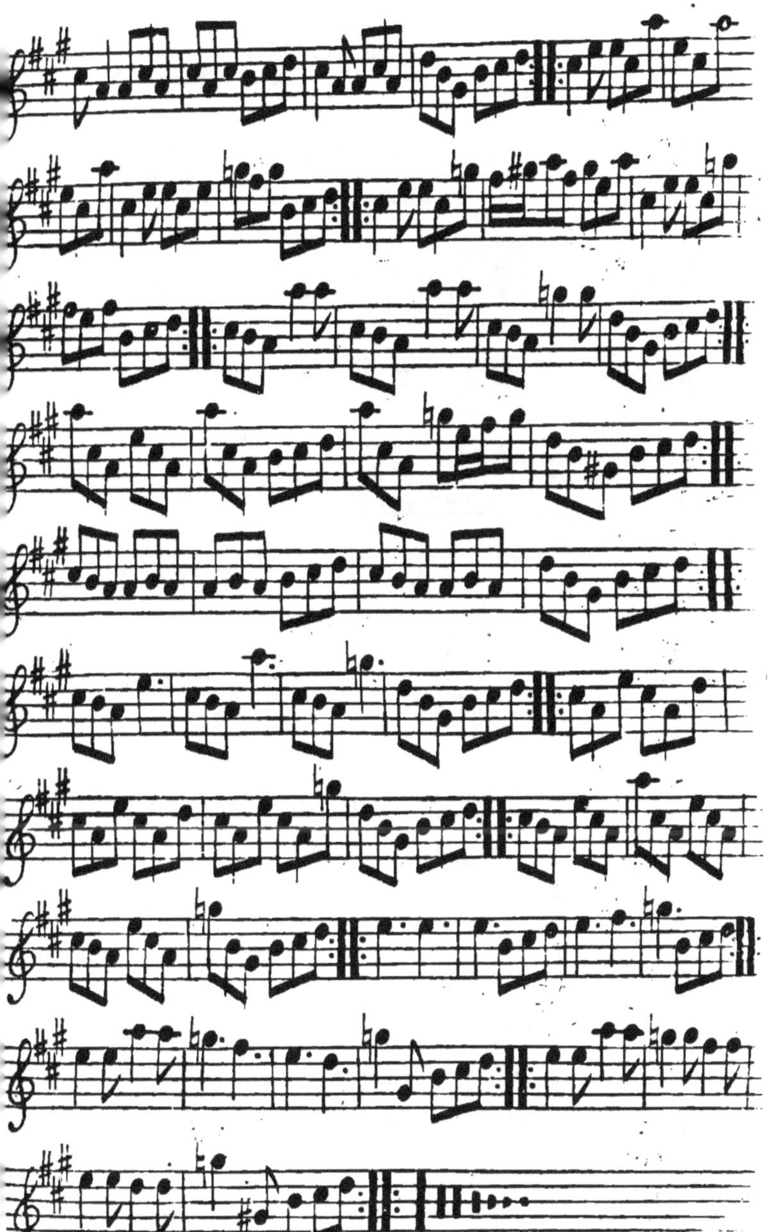

Drimen Duff.

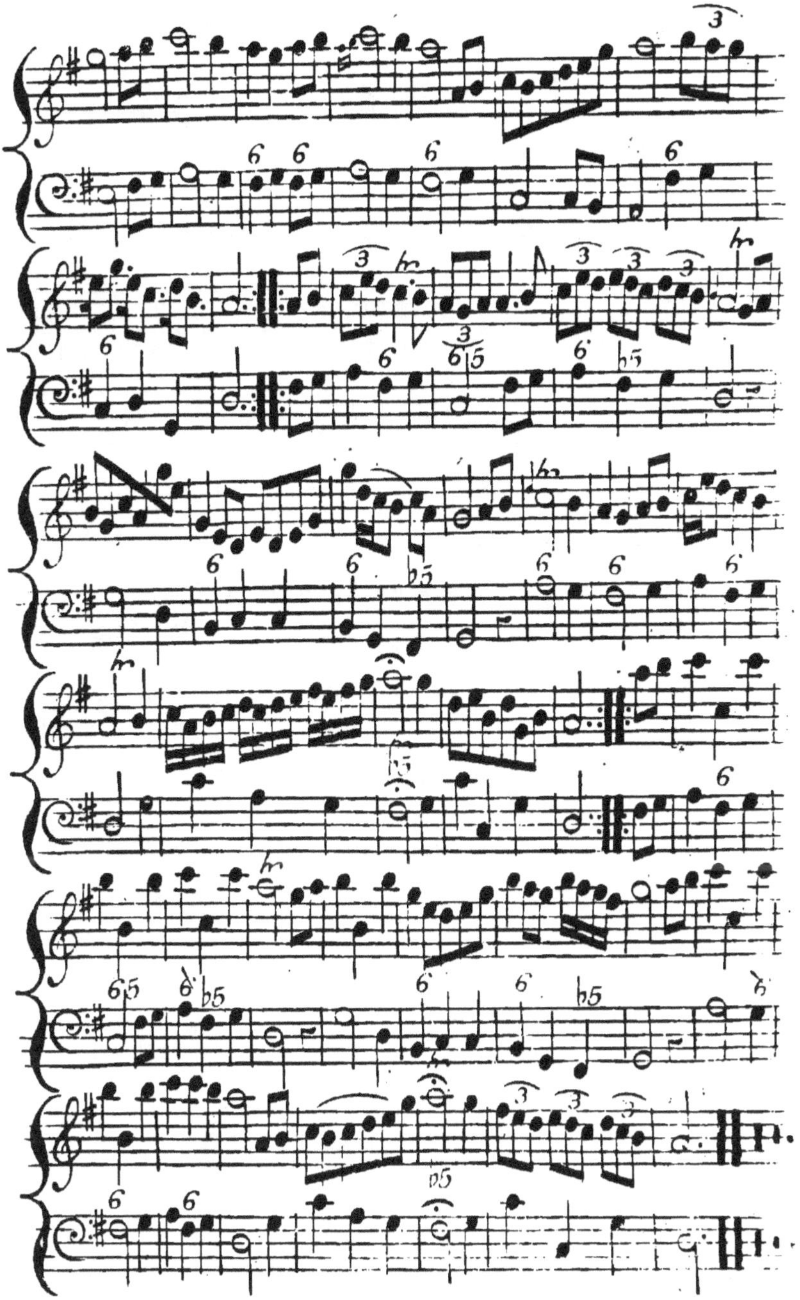

Curri Koun Dilich

N°. XX

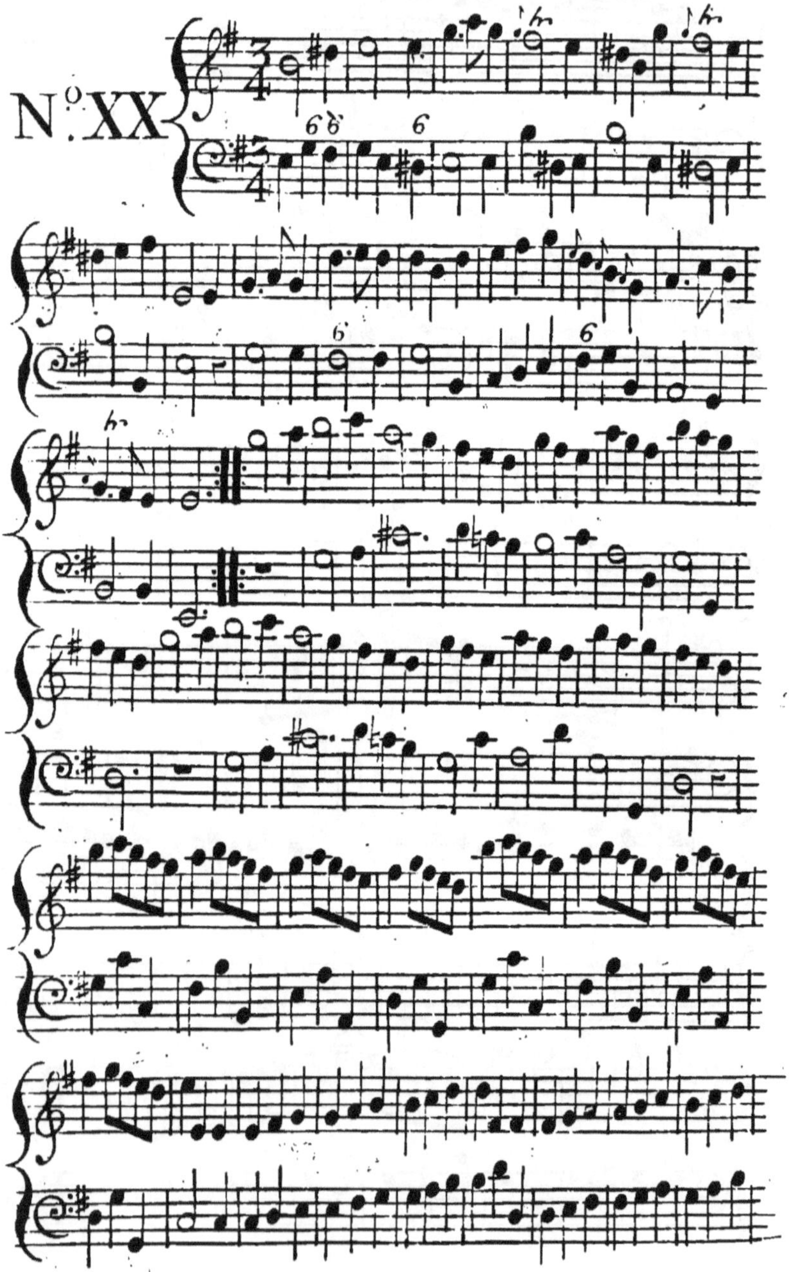

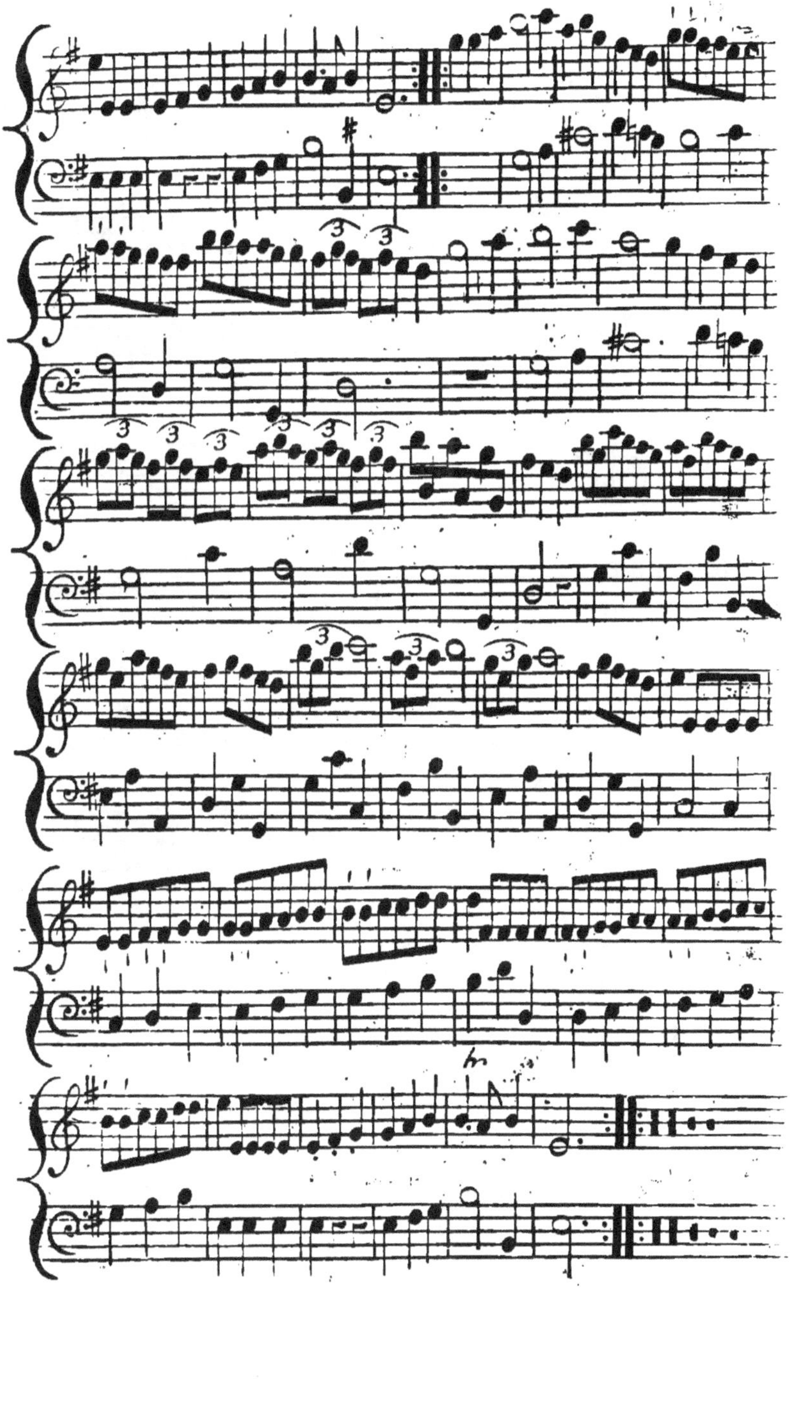

Mr. Creagh's Irish Tune.

No XXI

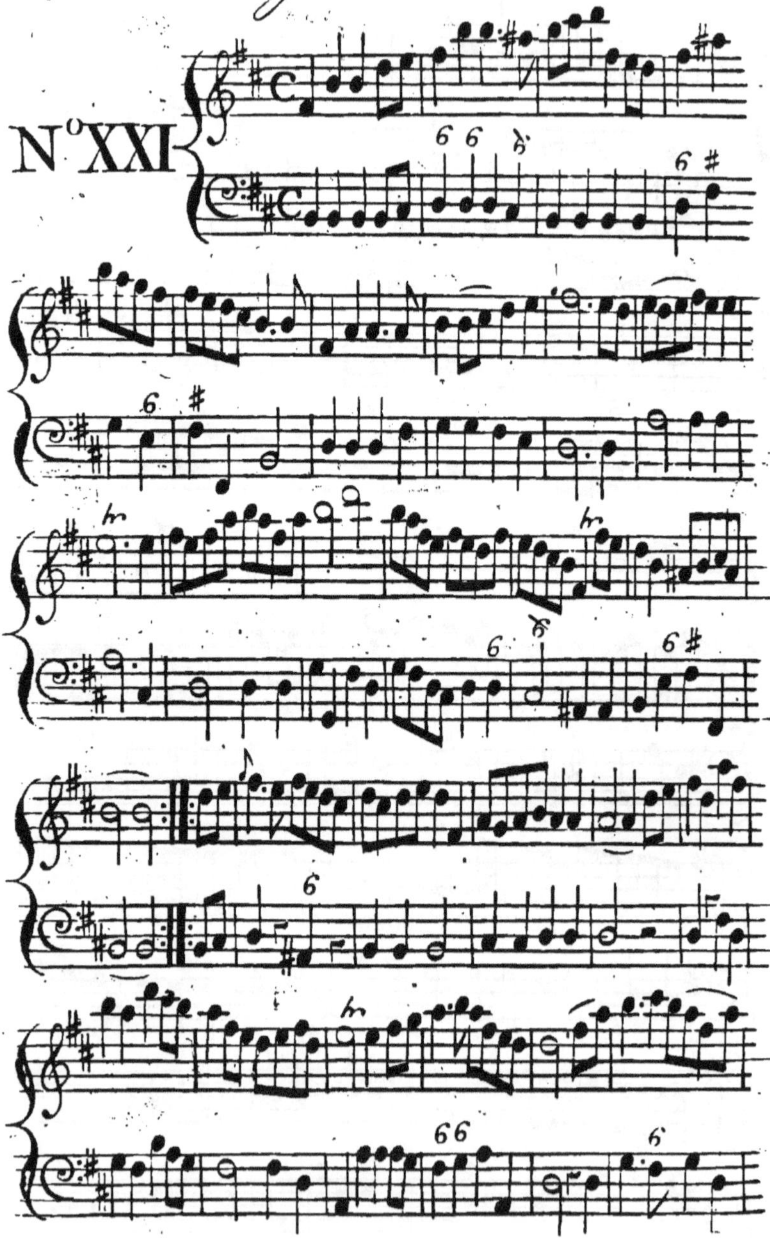

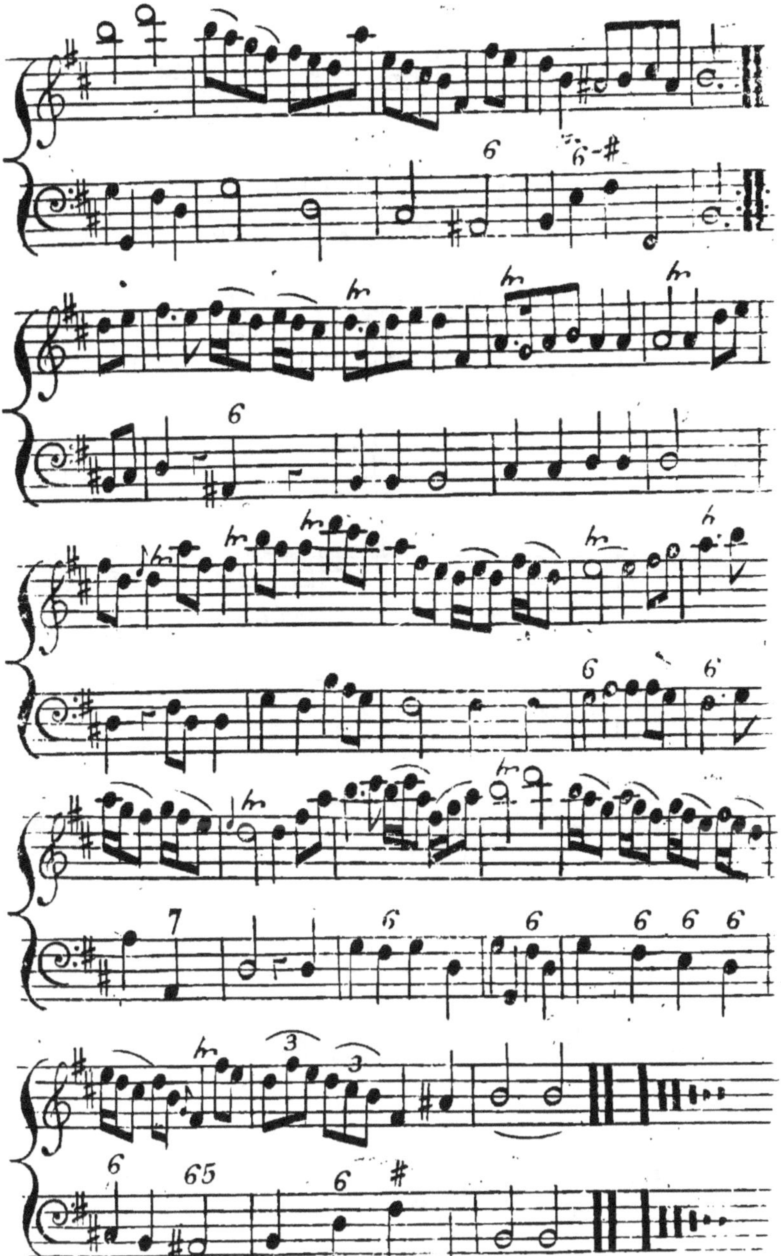

Hugar. Mu Fean.

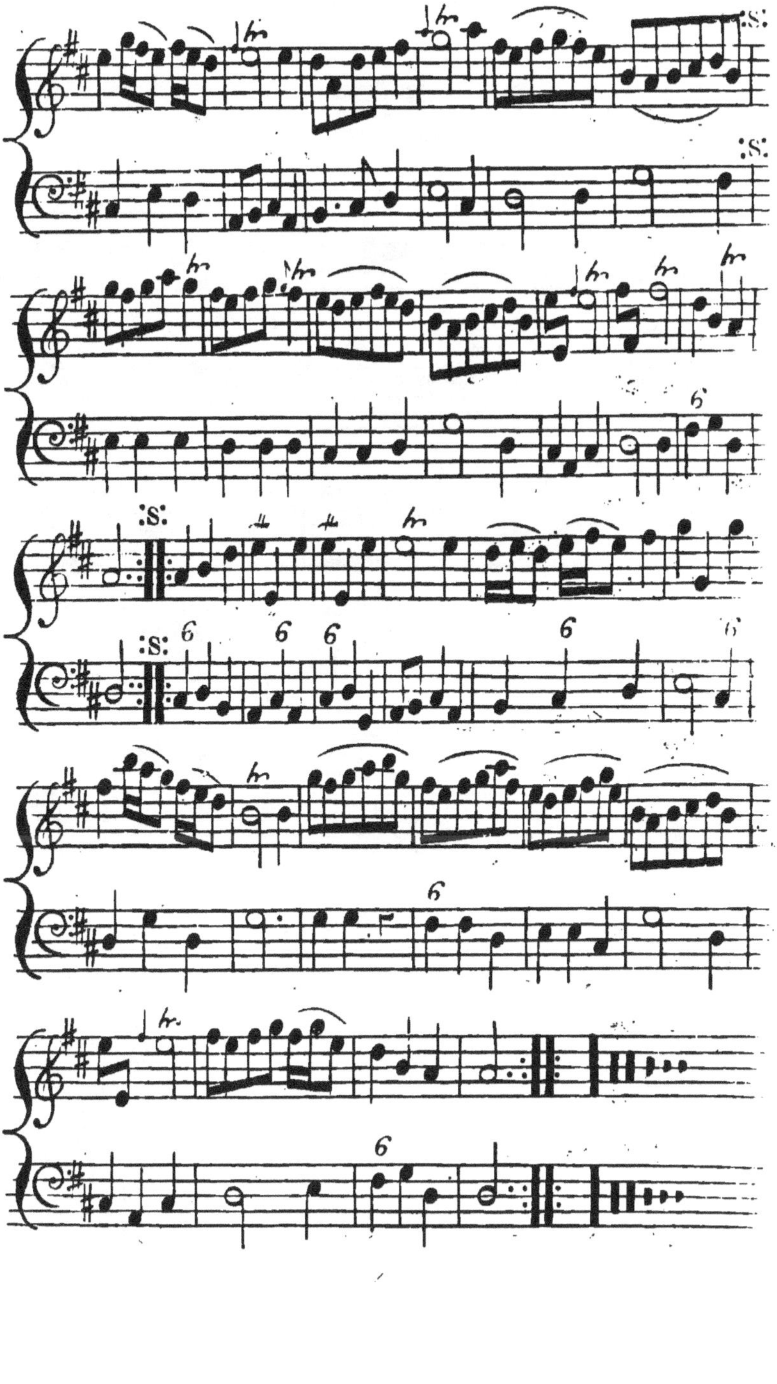

The Irish Cry.

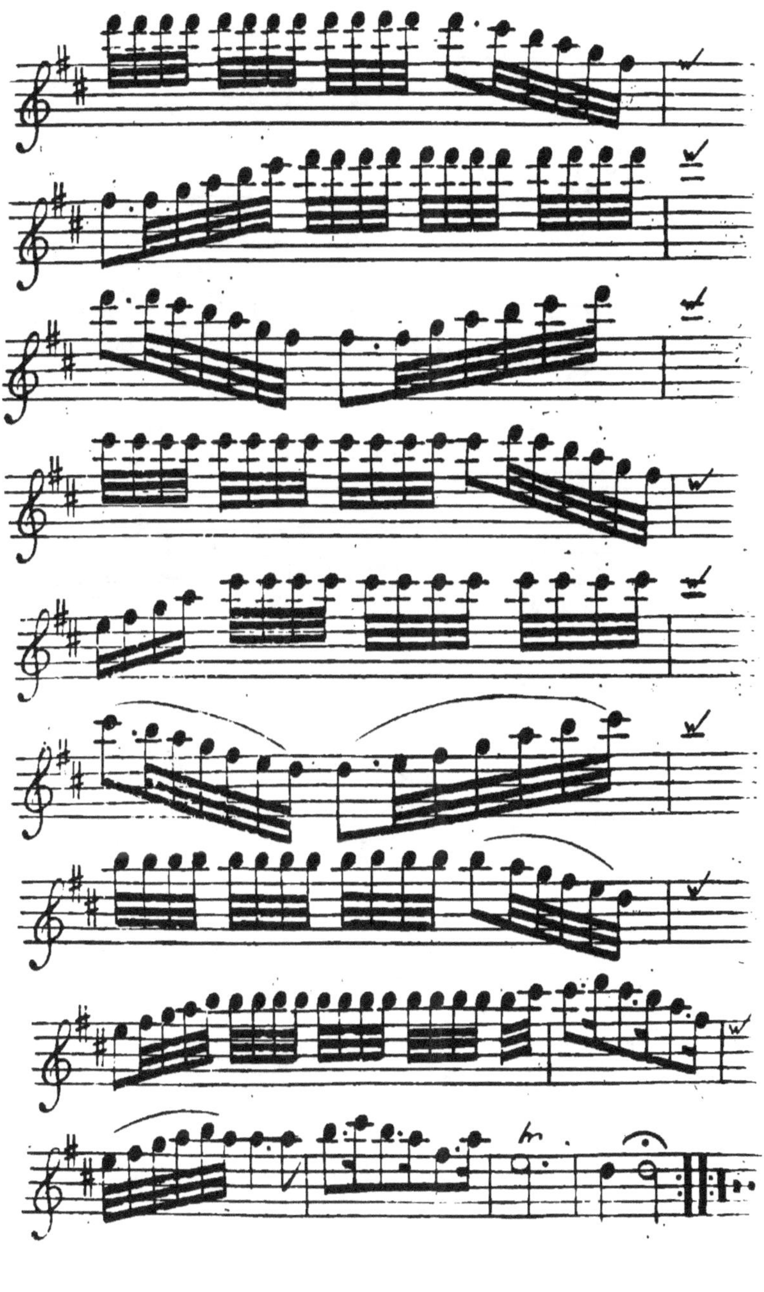

Jigg to the Irish Cry.

N.º XXIV.

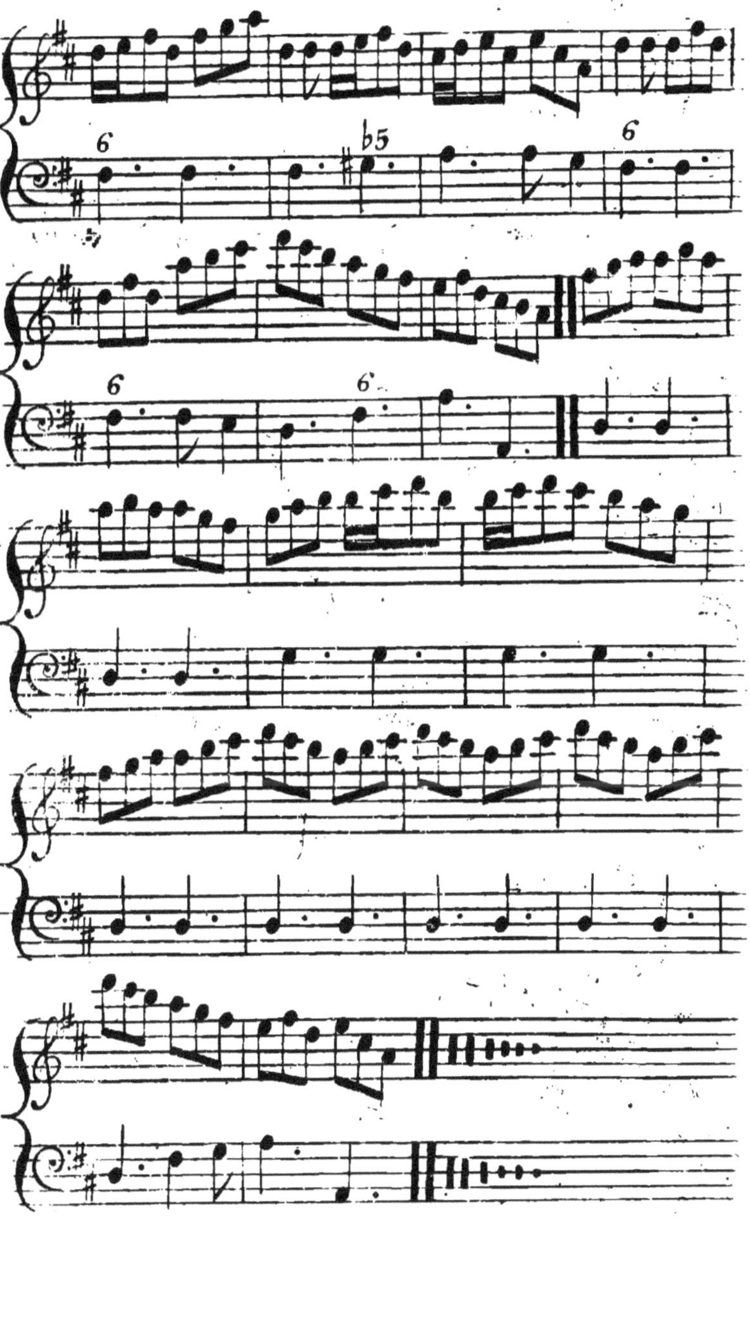
6
♭5
6
6
6

www.ingramcontent.com/pod-product-compliance
Lightning Source LLC
Chambersburg PA
CBHW021553270326
41931CB00009B/1190